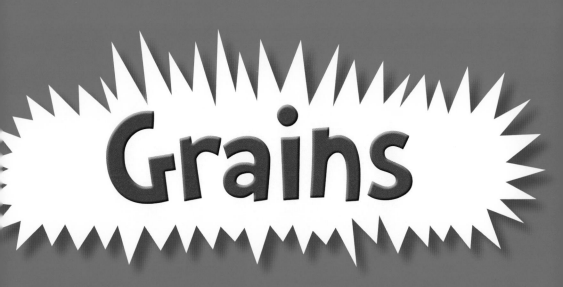

Grains

BY ALLISON LASSIEUR

amicus
high interest

Amicus High Interest is an imprint of Amicus
P.O. Box 1329, Mankato, MN 56002
www.amicuspublishing.us

Library of Congress Cataloging-in-Publication Data
Lassieur, Allison, author.
 Grains / by Allison Lassieur.
     pages cm. – (Where does our food come from?)
 Summary: "Describes grains, an essential part of a healthy
diet, including where different varieties are grown, why they
are healthy for us, and how other parts of the world consume
grains"– Provided by publisher.
 Audience: K to grade 3.
 Includes bibliographical references and index.
 ISBN 978-1-60753-497-6 (library binding) –
 ISBN 978-1-60753-704-5 (ebook)
 1. Grain–Juvenile literature. 2. Food supply–Juvenile literature.
I. Title.
 SB189.L26 2015
 664.7–dc23
                                        2013034691

Editors: Rebecca Glaser and Tram Bui
Series Designer: Kathleen Petelinsek
Book Designer: Heather Dreisbach
Photo Researcher: Kurtis Kinneman

Photo credits: Shutterstock, cover; Christine Langer-Pueschel/
Shutterstock, 5; Anna_Huchak/Shutterstock, 6; Brian Young/
Alamy, 9; scenery2/Shutterstock, 10; XiXinXing/Shutterstock,
13; Terrance Emerson/Shutterstock, 14; rtbilder/Shutterstock,
17; Inga Spence/Alamy, 18–19; Diana Taliun/Shutterstock,
21; sohadiszno/Shutterstock, 22; Hurst Photo/Shutterstock,
25; Imagebroker.net/SuperStock, 26–27; Exactostock/
SuperStock, 28

Printed in the United States of America at Corporate Graphics
in North Mankato, Minnesota.

10 9 8 7 6 5 4 3 2 1

Table of Contents

What Are Grains?

Did you know that **grains** are grass seeds? A grain is the seed of a grassy plant that you can eat. Wheat, rice, and corn are seeds, or grains. So are barley and oats. Foods like bread, pasta, and tortillas are made from grains. Anything made from grains is part of the grains food group.

There are many types of grains.

A stalk of wheat has many seeds.

 How much grain should you eat?

Each grain seed, or kernel, has three parts. The outer layer is the bran. It has lots of **fiber**. In the middle is the endosperm. This is what most flour is made from. A small part inside is the germ. The germ is the healthiest part.

 Kids should eat 5 ounces (142 g) of grains each day. One pancake, one slice of bread, or 3 cups of popcorn count as 1 ounce (28 g).

How many types of bread have you noticed? Some are made with **whole grains**. These foods use all three parts of the grain. Bread baked with **refined grains** uses only the endosperm. This makes the flour soft and easy to use. But it also gets rid of many vitamins and **nutrients**.

 What foods are made with grains?

Breads made with whole grains are usually darker in color.

 Oatmeal, pretzels, crackers, and corn chips are just a few.

Rice grows best in hot, wet fields.

Who eats more of the grain supply: people or animals?

Where Do Grains Grow?

Grains grow around the world. Some grains, such as corn, grow better in warm summer weather. Rye crops grow best in cold winter weather. Rice grows well where it is hot and wet all year long. Wheat grows where there are warm summers and cold winters. Grains are gathered in the fall.

 People! We eat one-half of the grain supply. One-third of the grain goes to animals. The rest is used to make fuels and other industrial goods.

Grains are a **staple food**. They are a big part of people's diets. A staple food is one that people eat every day. They can be eaten in many ways. You can bake fresh bread or have rice with dinner. You can mix wheat noodles with sauce, veggies, and meat. Rice, corn, and wheat are staple grains everywhere.

 Wait a minute. Is corn a vegetable or a grain?

Rice is a staple food that many people eat.

 Both! If you eat fresh corn, you are eating a vegetable. When corn is dried, like popcorn, it is a grain.

Yellow corn is grown in the U.S.

Traveling Grains

The U.S. grows most of its own grains. Wheat grows in the Midwest. Rice grows in southern states. Corn grows almost anywhere. The U.S. grows more corn than any other place in the world. A lot of it is **exported** to countries like Russia, Japan, and South Korea.

People eat a lot of grains. But animals do, too. Cows, pigs, fish, and chickens eat corn. Farmers like to feed grains to their animals. It makes them grow faster. Some corn from the U.S. is exported to feed animals. It may be sent overseas to feed cows in Europe or chickens in Africa.

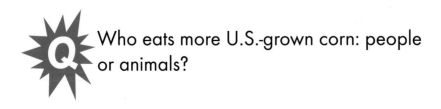

Who eats more U.S.-grown corn: people or animals?

Chickens eat grains so they can grow.

 Animals! Nearly 40 percent of U.S. corn feeds animals. The rest is used as food, fuel, and other goods.

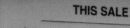

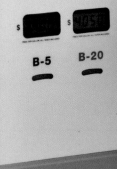

Most people eat grains every day. But grains are not always used as food! Corn can be made into fuel for cars. Grains can be used to make things in your house. Paint, crayons, and candles can be made with corn.

Some cars use fuel that is made from corn.

Grains Around the World

People around the world eat many kinds of grains. If you live in Peru, you might eat kaniwa (kan-yee-wah). It is a tiny grain that is packed with vitamins. Quinoa (kee-NO-wah) comes from South America. It is cooked like rice. In Ethiopia, people make bread from teff. It has a lot of protein. Teff also has a nutty taste.

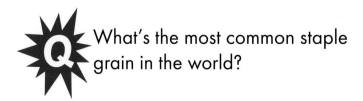

What's the most common staple grain in the world?

Quinoa is a grain that can be red or white.

 Rice! People in Asia eat rice with almost every meal.

People have grown grains for thousands of years. Some **ancient** grains are still eaten today. Kamut is from ancient Egypt. It has a buttery taste. The Aztecs ate foods made with amaranth grain. It has a deep peppery taste. Today it is popped as popcorn. Spelt grains were used in ancient Rome. You can still buy spelt bread today.

Spelt grains have been grown since ancient times. They are still used today to make bread.

Healthy Grains

The grains food group is more than just bread. Breakfast cereals are made from corn, wheat, oats, and rice. Pasta and granola are made from grain, too. Try to eat foods made from whole grains. Whole grains are better for you. Look for the words "whole grain" on the label.

Grains can be used to make many kinds of foods.

Why are grains so important? Grains are filled with vitamins and nutrients. They can help your body fight disease. Whole grains have fiber. Fiber helps your body digest food. Grains have lots of iron, which is good for the blood. Plus they taste good.

Eating grains can help you stay healthy.

Whole grain cereal with raisins is a great breakfast.

 **Q** How can you tell if a food is made with whole grain?

How much grain should you eat? About one-fourth of your plate should be filled with grain. Eat whole grains. Try whole-wheat bread instead of white bread. Eat brown rice instead of white rice. Use whole grain flour in cakes and cookies. Snack on toasted oat bars. Grains are part of a healthy diet.

 Read the label. Some foods may look like they have whole grains. But the color might be from other ingredients.

Glossary

ancient Very old, from a long time ago.

export To send products to another country to be sold there.

fiber A part of some foods that passes through the body, but is not digested.

grain The seeds of a cereal plant.

nutrient A chemical that is needed by people, animals, and plants to stay strong and healthy.

refined grain A grain used in foods that has the bran and germ taken out.

staple food Any food eaten regularly that makes up the greatest portion of a country's diet.

whole grain A grain used in foods that uses all three parts of the grain seed.

Read More

Cleary, Brian P. *Macaroni and Rice and Bread by the Slice: What Is in the Grains Group?* Minneapolis: Millbrook Press, 2011.

Reinke, Beth. *The Grains Group.* Mankato, Minn.: Child's World, 2013.

Schuh, Mari. *Grains On MyPlate.* Mankato, Minn.: Capstone Press, 2013.

Websites

Eating Well with Canada's Food Guide
www.hc-sc.gc.ca/fn-an/food-guide-aliment/index-eng.php

Kids' Nutrition Games
www.nourishinteractive.com/kids/5-food-group-games

MyPlate Kids' Place
www.choosemyplate.gov/kids/index.html

Index

About the Author

Allison Lassieur tries to eat plenty of fresh, good foods at every meal. She has written more than 100 books for kids. Allison especially likes to write about history, food, and science. She lives in a house in the woods with her husband, daughter, three dogs, two cats, and a blue fish named Marmalade.